WILD ANIMAL PLANET

ANIMAL HABITATS

COMPARE WHERE REPTILES, MAMMALS, SHARKS, BIRDS AND
INSECTS LIVE AND HOW THEY ADAPT TO THEIR ENVIRONMENTS

CONSULTANT: MICHAEL CHINERY

southwater

This edition is published by Southwater, an imprint of Anness Publishing Ltd, Hermes House, 88–89 Blackfriars Road, London SE1 8HA; tel. 020 7401 2077; fax 020 7633 9499

www.southwaterbooks.com; www.annesspublishing.com

If you like the images in this book and would like to investigate using them for publishing, promotions or advertising, please visit our website www.practicalpictures.com for more information.

UK agent: The Manning Partnership Ltd; tel. 01225 478444; fax 01225 478440; sales@manning-partnership.co.uk
UK distributor: Grantham Book Services Ltd; tel. 01476 541080; fax 01476 541061; orders@gbs.tbs-ltd.co.uk
North American agent/distributor: National Book Network; tel. 301 459 3366; fax 301 429 5746; www.nbnbooks.com
Australian agent/distributor: Pan Macmillan Australia; tel. 1300 135 113; fax 1300 135 103; customer.service@macmillan.com.au
New Zealand agent/distributor: David Bateman Ltd; tel. (09) 415 7664; fax (09) 415 8892

Publisher: Joanna Lorenz
Managing Editor: Linda Fraser
Editor: Rebecca Clunes
Editorial Reader: Penelope Goodare
Authors: Michael Bright, John Farndon, Robin Kerrod, Rhonda Klevansky, Dr Jen Green, Barbara Taylor
Illustrators: Julian Baker, Peter Bull, Vanessa Card, Linden Artists, Stuart Carter, Rob Sheffield, Sarah Smith, David Webb

ETHICAL TRADING POLICY
Because of our ongoing ecological investment program, you, as our customer, can have the pleasure and reassurance of knowing that a tree is being cultivated on your behalf to naturally replace the materials used to make the book you are holding. For further information about this scheme, go to www.annesspublishing.com/trees

Picture credits
ABPL: 32tl, 33bl, 33cl, 33br, 37br / Daryl Balfour: 34b, 35t / Clem Haagner: 45cr / Dave Hamman: 45t / Gerald Hinde 35bl / Gavin Tomson: 35br; **Animals Animals:** 58ct; **Ardea London:** Stefan Meyers: 50b / Brian and Cherry Alexander: 48t / Francois Gohier: 52t / M Krishnan: 53tl; **Bridgeman Art Library:** 53br; **Ancient Art and Architecture Collection:** 22br / Ken Lucas: 29tl; **Heather Angel:** 38tr, 41ll, 41tr, 43tl, 43br; **BBC Natural History Unit:** 23t, 31br / Christopher Becker: 49tr / Gerry Ellis: 41bl /D Hall: 63cl / Andrew Harrington: 49tl / Simon King: 52br / P Oxford: 25br, 28bl, 53tr / Michael W Richards: 55tr; **Adam Britton:** 24tr; **Bruce Coleman:** 16bl, 16br, 19tr, 20cr, 20b, 26bl, 34r, 36cr, 50bl, 59t / I Arndt: 10c, 12bl, 53tl / Erwin and Peggy Bauer: 46b / RIM Campbell: 57tl / Alain Compost: 34tr, 45tl & cl/ G Dore 10bl / P Evans: 11bl / Jose Luis Gonzalez Grande: 28tl / L C Marigo: 25c / Joe Mcdonald: 43b/ Dieter and Mary Plage: 15tr, 55b / Andrew Purcell: 14b / K Taylor: 10tr / Rod Williams: 45tr; **Mary Evans:** 19br, 42tr, 45cl; **FLPA:** 12br, 13cr, 15c, 18b, 18r, 20–21, 21bl, 42b / M Harvey: 54tl / JJ Hinojosa: 26tr; **Gallo Images:** 27tr / Nigel Dennis: 27br / Thomas Dressler: 32tl, 33bl, 33cl, 33br; **Holt Studios International:** 16tr; **Innerspace Visions:** 62tl / D Perrine: 60br, 61bl, 62br / JD Watt: 61br; **National Geographic:** 60tl / N Calogianis: 61tl; **Natural Science Photos:** 37tr / D Allen: 42t; **NHPA:** 6t, 7br, 8t, 9b, 17tl, 17cl, 17bl, 19c, 20tl, 21tl, 25t, 30bl, 37bl, 39br, 58bl, 63tl / Nigel Dennis: 32b / Christopher Ratier: 54bl / Andy Rouse: 44t / Jany Sauvanet: 51cl /Mirko Stelzner: 51t / Philip Ware: 34c; **Oxford Scientific Films:** 7t, 9t, 9c, 30br, 36bl, 38bl, 40tl, 40br, 43br, 43cl, 51cr, 58cr, 59b, 58b, 59t, 59bl / Martyn Colbeck: 34bl / R Davies: 23b / David B Fleetham: 29br, 60cl / Mark Hamblin: 27cr / H Hall: 61cr / Mike Hill: 50t / Frank Huber: 38br / M Leach: 29cl / Joe Mcdonald: 53bl / Overseas: 51b / S Osolinski: 23c / M Pitts: 24b / Andrew Plumptre: 55cr, 56br, 57tr / Norbert Rosing: 29tr / Krupaker Senani: 47c / Peter Weiman: 47b; **Papilio:** 8br, 15tl, 47bl; **Planet Earth:** 27cl, 33tl, 37cl, 43tr, 47br, 50t, 57bl, 59c / K Lucas: 22t/ M Price: 22bl; **Premaphotos Wildlife:** 14t, 15b; **Stouffer Productions:** 40br; **Kim Taylor:** 6b; **Visual Arts Library:** Artepot Roland: 11br; **Warren Photographic:** 7bl, 8bl / Kim Taylor: 13tl, cl, & br; **Zefa Pictures:** 21br

Contents

A Place to Live

Ever since life began, different species have competed with each other for food and living space. This competition has led to each kind of animal becoming more or less specialized for a particular way of life in certain surroundings, known as its habitat, which may be a woodland, a savanna grassland, a small pond or a vast ocean. Wherever it lives, the animal must be well suited to its habitat, otherwise it will not survive. Most animals keep to one kind of habitat, but some species can survive in different surroundings, so long as they can find food.

Wolves can live in a range of habitats, from forests to open areas. Most wolves live in cool, temperate parts of the world, but some live in the deserts of south-east Asia.

Weather conditions

The climate – the temperature and amount of rainfall in an area – is the major factor that determines whether animals can exist in a particular place. Life cannot exist where the temperature is permanently below 15°F or above 115°F, but there are species that survive at all temperatures between these limits. Bears and other mammals living in very cold places generally have thick fur to keep them warm, while whales living in cold seas have a thick layer of body fat, called blubber, beneath the skin. Some insects living in cold regions have a kind of antifreeze in their blood to prevent them from freezing solid.

Animals living in deserts have usually adapted their behavior to cope with the difficult conditions. Many hide away in burrows in the heat of the day and come out only at night when the air is cooler. Beetles that roam about by day often have long legs to keep their bodies off the burning hot sand.

The grey whale migrates some 6,000 miles between its summer feeding grounds and winter breeding grounds. Many other animals also migrate in order to find the perfect habitat.

All living things need water to survive, and this is a particular problem for animals that live in deserts. Most have internal adaptations to help them use water more efficiently. Some desert animals never need to drink because they get enough water from their food and use it very carefully.

Snakes are found in many different sorts of habitat, from deserts to rainforests. Most snakes can only live in warm climates, however, as they need the sun's heat to maintain their body temperature.

Enough to eat

Climate is not the only thing that determines where an animal can live. Within a region of suitable climate, animals can survive only where they can find the right habitat, with the right kinds of plants or other animals to eat.

Animals search for their food in several ways. Some animals or family groups of animals, such as elephants, roam freely through a habitat without having any fixed home. Most animals, however, keep within a certain area. A pride (group) of lions, for example, has a definite territory that it defends against other lions. A territory may be large or small, but it will be big enough to provide food for all the animals living in the group, and it will have somewhere safe for the animals to raise their young.

Summer and winter – the changing seasons

The cool and temperate regions of the world experience very different conditions in summer and winter. Many mammals cope with the change by growing thicker coats for winter, but some move to warmer places. Several kinds of whale make these long-distance journeys, which are called migrations. They move to tropical waters for the winter and have their babies, and then go back to the cooler waters in spring. But cold weather is not the only problem facing animals in winter. Food may be in short supply, especially in areas that get a lot of snow. Some animals, including the raccoon dog, overcome this problem by hibernating (sleeping through the winter). They gorge themselves in the summer, building up a layer of fat to help them survive the winter.

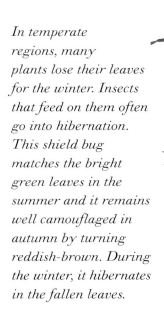

In temperate regions, many plants lose their leaves for the winter. Insects that feed on them often go into hibernation. This shield bug matches the bright green leaves in the summer and it remains well camouflaged in autumn by turning reddish-brown. During the winter, it hibernates in the fallen leaves.

Success story

Animals have been incredibly successful at adapting to different habitats and environments. Today, there is hardly any place on Earth – from the highest mountain peaks to the deepest oceans – that does not support some kind of animal life.

Beetle and Bug Environments

Our planet has a huge number of different habitats, and beetles and bugs are found in most of them. Like other insects, beetles and bugs usually live in hot, tropical regions or in mild, temperate areas. Some, though, can survive on snow-capped mountains or frozen icefields, in caves and even in hot springs. Other beetles and bugs are found in places with heavy rainfall, and a few tough species survive in deserts.

Beetles and bugs that live in very cold or very hot places often adapt their life cycle to cope with the extreme temperatures. Many survive the coldest or driest periods as eggs in the soil. In deserts, beetles and bugs tend to be active at night, when the air is cooler. The toughest species have adapted to survive for long periods without food or even water.

▲ **A WARM HOME**
Bedbugs are parasites that live and feed on warm-blooded animals. Some species suck human blood while others infest the homes of birds and furry mammals, or live among their feathers or fur. Kept warm by their host animal, some bedbugs can even survive in cold places such as the Arctic.

Did you know? Water boatmen can fly many miles to find a new home.

◀ **LIFE IN THE WATER**
Water boatmen are predatory bugs that have adapted to life in the water. They prey on all kinds of small water creatures, including tadpoles and tiny fish. They are also called backswimmers because they swim upside-down, using their long back legs rather like oars. The bugs come to the surface from time to time to renew their air supplies.

LIVING IN THE DARK ▶

This stilt-legged bug has adapted to pitch-black caves in the Caribbean. Its antennae and legs are long and thin, to help it to feel its way. The legs and antennae are also covered with hairs that can detect the slightest air currents, alerting the bug to the presence of other animals.

◀ DESERT SURVIVOR

The fog-basking beetle lives in the Namib Desert, in southern Africa. This beetle has an ingenious way of drinking. When fog and mist swirl over the dunes, it does a handstand and points its abdomen in the air. Moisture gathers on its body, then trickles down special grooves on its back into its waiting mouth.

NO CAMOUFLAGE REQUIRED ▶

This *Aphaenops* beetle lives in caves high in the Pyrenees mountains, between France and Spain. Its body is not well camouflaged but, in the dark of the caves, disguise is not important. Scientists believe some cave-dwelling species developed from beetles that first lived in the caves during the last Ice Age, about a million years ago.

◀ DUNE DWELLER

The dune beetle lives in the deserts of southern Africa. It is one of the few white beetles. White reflects the rays of the sun and helps to keep the insect cool. The pale color also blends in well with the sand where it lives, which helps it to hide from predators. The beetle's wing cases are hard and close-fitting, and so help to conserve precious body moisture in this dry region. Long legs raise the beetle's body above the burning hot desert sand.

dune beetle
(Onymacris bicolor)

Insects Living

Some beetles and bugs live in and on fresh water – not only ponds and rivers but also icy lakes, muddy pools and stagnant marshes. Different types of water-dwellers live at different depths. Some live on or just below the water surface. Other species swim in the mid-depths, or lurk in the mud or sand at the bottom. Beetles and bugs that live underwater carry a supply of air down with them so that they can breathe.

In some other insects, only the larvae (young) live in the water, where there is plenty of food. The adults live on land.

SURFACE SPINNERS

Whirligig beetles are oval, flattened beetles that live on the surface of ponds and streams. Their eyes are divided into two, so that they can see above and below the water at the same time. The beetles are named after a spinning toy called a whirligig, because they swim in circles.

SKATING ON WATER

Pond skaters live on the water surface. They move about like ice skaters on their long slender legs. The bugs' feet make dimples on the surface of the water, but do not break it. When the bugs sense a drowning insect nearby, they skate over in gangs to feed on it.

SPINY STRAW

A water scorpion has a long, hollow spine on its abdomen. The spine has no sting, but it is used to suck air from the surface. Sensors on the spine tell the bug when it is too deep to breathe.

In and On Water

THE AQUATIC SCORPION

Water scorpions are fierce predators. This bug has seized a stickleback fish in its pincer-like front legs. It then uses its mouthparts to pierce the fish's skin and suck out its juices. Compared to some aquatic insects, water scorpions are not strong swimmers. They usually move about by crawling slowly over submerged plants.

DIVING DEEP

Saucer bugs are expert divers. In order to breathe, the bug takes in air through spiracles (holes) in its body. Tiny bubbles of air are also trapped between the bug's body hairs, giving it its silvery color. Saucer bugs use their front legs to grab their prey. They cannot fly, but move from pond to pond by crawling through the grass.

UNDERWATER ROWING

You can often see lesser water boatmen just below the water surface, but they can also dive further down. They use their back legs to row underwater, and breathe air trapped under their wings. The females lay their eggs on water plants or glue them to stones on the stream bed. The eggs hatch two months later.

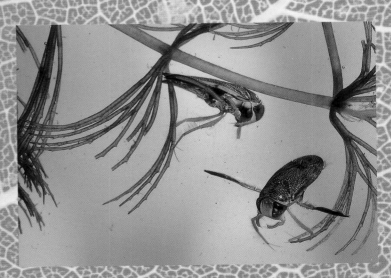

Butterfly Habitats

Almost every country in the world has its own particular range of butterflies and moths. They are surprisingly adaptable insects, and inhabit a huge variety of different environments, from the fringes of deserts to icy Arctic areas.

Butterflies and moths that live in cold climates tend to be darker than those living in warmer regions. This is because they need to be warm in order to fly, and dark colors soak up sunlight more easily. In mountainous areas, the local species usually fly close to the ground. Flying any higher than this would create a risk of being blown away by strong gusts of wind. Some female moths living in mountainous areas do not have wings at all, and move around by crawling along the ground.

orange-tip
butterfly
(*Anthocharis
cardamines*)

**◄ HEDGEROWS
AND WAYSIDES**
Orange-tip butterflies, named for the bright orange tips of the male's front wings, live in a wide range of grassy places, including hedgerows, woodland margins, damp meadows and roadsides. When at rest, with their front wings hidden behind the hind wings, their mottled green undersides blend in with the vegetation and make them very difficult to see.

apollo butterfly
(*Parnassius apollo*)

◄ HIGH LIFE
The apollo butterfly has adapted to life in the mountains of Europe and Asia. The apollo's body is covered with fur-like scales that protect it from the extreme cold. Most apollo eggs that are laid in autumn do not hatch until the following spring because of the low temperatures. Those caterpillars that do hatch hibernate at once.

◄ WETLAND WANDERER
The marsh fritillary butterfly flourishes among the flowers of open grassland in temperate regions (areas with warm summers and cold winters). It is happy in both damp and dry areas, but it needs plenty of warm sunshine in the spring to enable its caterpillars to develop properly.

BUTTERFLY HABITATS ▶

Some butterflies, such as the large white, occur in many habitats, including backyards. Others are more choosy about their homes. The grayling and Spanish festoon like coastal areas, while the speckled wood and white admiral prefer woodland glades. Arctic species include the moorland clouded yellow. The apollo and Cynthia's fritillary are alpine butterflies living high in mountains. Painted ladies inhabit many areas in summer, but spend the winter around the deserts of North Africa.

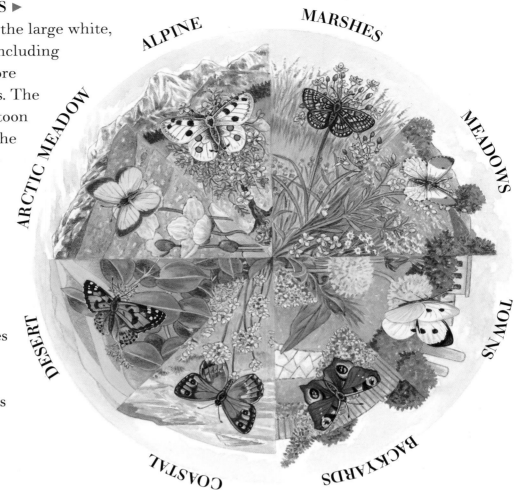

ALPINE MARSHES MEADOWS TOWNS BACKYARDS COASTAL DESERT ARCTIC MEADOW

▼ GARDEN VISITORS

These peacock butterflies are feeding on a flower. Gardens provide food for all kinds of butterflies. Many flowers grown in gardens are related to wild roadside and field flowers.

The Warrior Symbol

A statue of a proud warrior stands at the ancient Toltec capital city of Tula in Mexico. An image of a butterfly appears on the warrior's breastplate. The Toltec people saw that butterflies live short but brilliant lives. Consequently, the butterfly became a symbol for Toltec soldiers who lived a brave, but often short, life and did not fear death.

11

Migrant Butterflies

Most butterflies and moths live and die within a very small area, never moving far from their birthplace. However, a few species travel astonishing distances in search of food, or to escape cold or overpopulated areas.

Some butterfly species, such as the painted lady and monarch, are true migrants, following the same routes year after year. For individual butterflies, however, it's a one-way trip. Clouded yellow caterpillars, for example, feed in the Mediterranean region in spring. As adults, many fly northwards to feed and mate. There, they lay eggs and new generations can be seen throughout the summer. But the clouded yellow cannot survive the cold and, apart from the few that manage to get back to southern Europe, the butterflies die in the autumn.

migration path

▲ THE ROYAL ROUTE

Monarch butterflies migrate mainly between North and Central America. Occasionally, instead of flying south, strong winds can sweep the butterflies 3,500 miles northeast, to Europe.

▲ TREE REST

Every autumn huge numbers of monarch butterflies leave Canada and the northern United States and fly 2,000 miles south to spend the winter in Mexico. They make the journey as quickly as possible, resting on trees on the way.

▲ MONARCHS ON THE MOVE

In spring, monarchs begin their journey north. They lay their eggs on the way and then die. Once their young become butterflies, the cycle begins again. The new butterflies either continue north or return south, depending on the season.

brown-veined white butterfly
(Belenois aurota)

◄ AN AFRICAN MIGRANT

This butterfly has large wings capable of carrying it over long distances. Millions of brown-veined white butterflies form swarms in many parts of southern Africa. A swarm can cause chaos to people attempting to drive through it. Although this butterfly flies throughout the year, the swarms are seen most often in December and January.

Did you know? A large swarm of migrating butterflies can bring farm machines to a standstill by resting on them.

FAST AS A HAWK ►

Every spring thousands of oleander hawk moths set off from their native lands in tropical Africa and head north, over the Mediterranean sea. A few of them reach the far north of Europe in late summer. Hawk moths are among the furthest flying of all moths. They are able to travel rapidly over long distances.

oleander hawk moth
(Daphnis nerii)

▲ SURVIVING THE COLD

The adult peacock butterfly hibernates during the winter. The peacock is protected by chemicals called glycols that stop its body fluids from freezing. Many other moths and butterflies survive the winter by hibernating instead of migrating.

▼ CHASING THE SUN

The painted lady butterfly lives almost all over the world. In summer it is found across Europe, as far north as Iceland. However, it cannot survive the winter frosts in temperate areas. Adults emerging in late summer head south, and a few reach North Africa before the autumn chill starts.

painted lady butterfly
(Vanessa cardui)

13

Spider Homes

There are few places on Earth that spiders do not live. They are found in forests, grasslands, marshes and deserts, on high mountain tops and hidden in caves. Even remote islands are inhabited by spiders, perhaps blown there on the wind or carried on floating logs. Many spiders live in our houses and some travel the world on cargo ships. Others make their home in city sewers, where there are plenty of flies for them to feed on. Spiders are not very common in watery places, however, as they cannot breathe underwater. There are no spiders in Antarctica, although some do live near the Arctic. To survive the winter in cool places, spiders may stay as eggs or hide under grass, rocks or bark. Some spiders even have a type of antifreeze to stop their bodies from freezing.

▲ HEDGEROW WEBS
One of the most common spiders on bushes and hedges in Europe and Asia is the hammock web spider. One hedge may contain thousands of webs with their haphazard threads.

Did you know? Some spiders live in the webs of other species of spider and steal their food.

◄ SPIDER IN THE SINK
The spiders that people sometimes find in the sink or the bathtub are usually male house spiders that have fallen in while searching for a mate. They cannot climb back up the smooth sides because they do not have gripping tufts of hair on their feet like hunting spiders.

▲ LURKING IN THE DARK

The cave orb-weaver almost always builds its web in very dark places, often suspended from the roof. It is found in caves, mines, hollow trees, railway tunnels, drains, wells and the corners of outbuildings in Europe, Asia and North America.

▲ LIVING IN A BURROW

The white lady spider lives in deserts. It hides away from the intense heat in a burrow beneath the sand. The main problem for desert spiders is lack of water. In times of drought the white lady spider may go into suspended animation, an extreme form of hibernation.

◄ HOSTILE HOME

This beach wolf spider is well camouflaged on the sand. It lives in a very hostile place. Waves pound on the beach and shift the sand. There is little fresh water and the sun quickly dries everything out. Food is scarce, although insects do gather on seaweed, rocks and plants growing along the edge of the shore.

RAINFOREST SPIDER ►

The greatest variety of spiders is found in tropical rainforests. Here, the climate is warm all year round and plenty of food is always available. This forest huntsman spider is well camouflaged against a tree trunk covered in lichen. To hide, it presses its body close against the tree. It lives in Malaysia where it is found in backyards as well as in the rainforest.

Snake Habitats

Every continent except Antarctica contains snakes, although they are most common in deserts and rainforests. Snakes cannot survive in very cold places because they use heat in the air around them to make their bodies work. Most snakes live in places where the temperature is high enough for them to stay active day and night. In cooler climates, snakes may spend the cold winter months asleep in hibernation.

▲ **OUT IN THE OPEN**
The European grass snake lives mainly on damp grassland. It sometimes climbs on to hedgerows to bask in the sunshine.

◄ **MOUNTAIN SURVIVAL**
The Pacific rattlesnake is sometimes found on the lower slopes of mountains in the western United States. In general, though, mountains are problem places for snakes because of their cold climates.

Pacific rattlesnake
(*Crotalus viridis*)

▲ **WINTER SLEEP**
Thousands of garter snakes emerge after their winter hibernation.

▼ **PLENTIFUL TROPICS**

Hot, tropical rainforests contain the greatest variety of snakes, including this Brazilian rainbow boa. There is plenty to eat in a rainforest, from insects, birds and bats to frogs.

▲ **FOREST LIFE**

This eyelash viper lives in the Central American rainforest. The climate here is warm all year round, so snakes can stay active all the time. Snakes have adapted to every niche provided by the rainforest – there are snakes in trees, on the forest floor, underground and in rivers.

Brazilian rainbow boa
(*Epicrates cenchria*)

BARK TUNNEL ▶

Yellow-headed worm snakes live under tree bark. Other worm snakes live underground where the soil is warm.

◀ **AT HOME IN THE DESERT**

This African puff adder lives in the deserts of southern Africa. Many snakes live in deserts because they can survive with little food and water.

17

Desert Snakes

Many snakes live in deserts, although the habitat is hot, dry and inhospitable. This is partly because snakes can survive for a long time without food. Mammals need energy from food to produce body heat, but reptiles take their heat from their surroundings. Snakes are also able to thrive in deserts because their waterproof skins stop them from losing too much water. During the hottest part of the day, and the bitterly cold nights, snakes shelter under rocks or in the ground — often in rodent burrows.

desert horned viper
(Cerastes cerastes)

▼ SCALE SOUND
If threatened, this viper makes a loud rasping sound by rubbing together jagged scales along the sides of its body. This warns predators to keep away.

► GO AWAY!
A rattlesnake warns enemies that it is dangerous by shaking the rattle in its tail. Desert snakes do not hiss because they would lose precious moisture through water vapor.

SAND SHUFFLER ▶

The desert horned viper is a master ambusher. It spreads its ribs to flatten its body and shuffles its way under the sand until it almost disappears and only its eyes and horns show. It strikes out at its prey from this position.

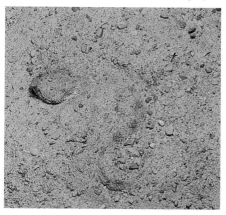

◀ DESERT MOVES

Many desert snakes, such as this Peringuey's viper, travel in a movement called sidewinding. As the snake moves, only a small part of its body touches the hot sand at any time. Sidewinding also helps to stop the snake sinking down into the loose sand.

◀ HIDDEN BOA

The colors of this sand boa make it hard for predators and prey to spot it among the rocks and sand. The snake's smooth, round body shape helps it to burrow down into the sand.

The Hopi Indians

This Native North American was a Hopi snake chief. The Hopi people used snakes in their rain dances to carry prayers to the rain gods to make rain fall on their desert lands.

Tropical

Near the Equator, in areas with plenty of sun and rain, tropical rainforests grow. They are dense jungles, teeming with life. The emerald tree boa lives in the rainforests of South America. Its green body is well camouflaged among the leaves. Like other tree snakes, it moves easily among the trees, at home high above the jungle floor.

UPSIDE-DOWN ATTACK

To catch a small mammal or bird, an emerald tree boa drapes its coils over a horizontal branch and hangs its head down. As soon as a victim comes within reach, it strikes. Once the snake has a firm hold with its teeth, it coils around its prey. The boa squeezes slowly until the animal stops breathing and dies. The snake swallows its victim head-first so that it slides down easily.

PATCHY OUTLINE

The creamy colored bands along the back of an emerald tree boa help to break up its outline and camouflage it in the dappled light.

SLIM SLITHERER

Tree boas are longer and slimmer than boas that live on the ground. Their streamlined shape and lightweight head help them to slither through the branches easily.

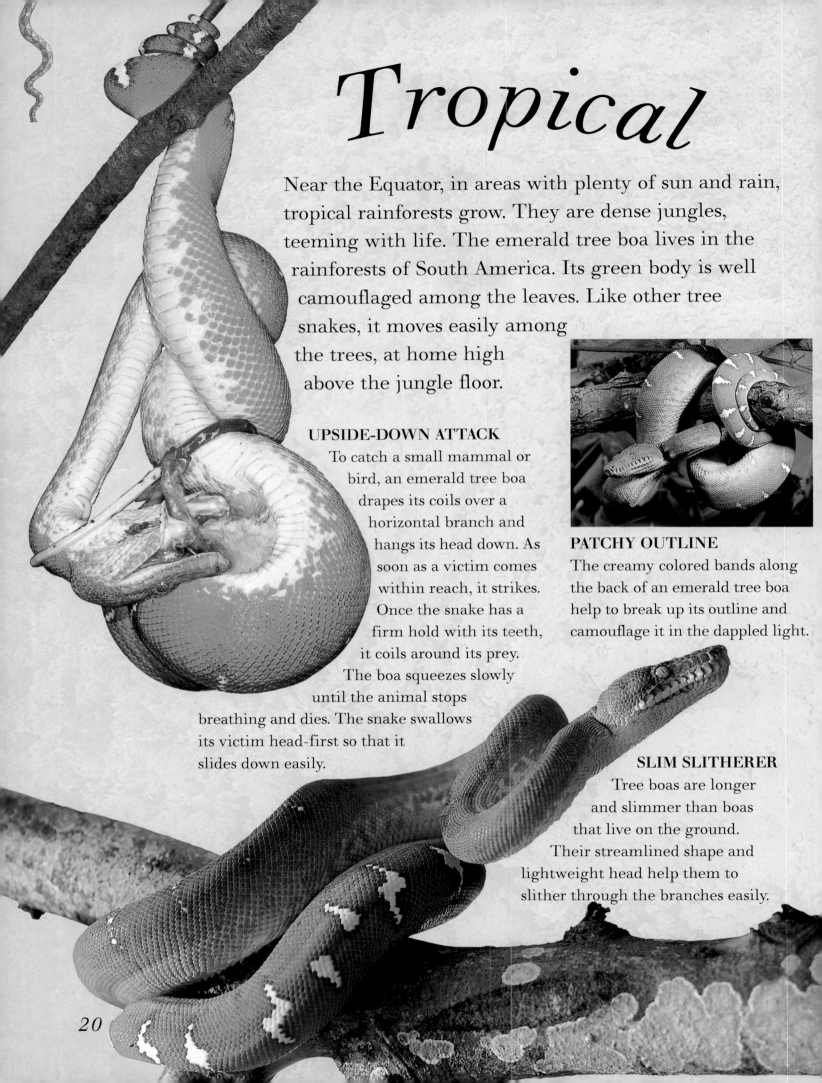

20

Tree Boas

emerald tree boa
(Corallus canina)

COLOR CHANGE

Young emerald tree boas are orange, pink or yellow when they are born. They gradually change to green in their first year by producing new color pigments in their skin. No one is sure why the young are a different color from the adults. They may live in different places and need their red coloring for effective camouflage.

HOT LIPS

Heat-sensitive areas on the tree boa's lips help it to detect the warm-blooded animals on which it feeds.

LETHAL JAWS

The emerald tree boa can open its mouth very wide to swallow prey. Its sharp teeth slope backwards to grip the victim firmly and stop it escaping.

21

Crocodiles of Rivers and Lakes

Most crocodiles, alligators and other crocodilians prefer fresh water to salty water. They live in rivers, lakes and swamps, in warm climates. Crocodilians tend to live at the edge of the water because the shallows provide many plants to hide among and plenty of animals to eat.

Water is helpful in other ways, too. Like other reptiles, crocodilians draw their heat from their surroundings. Water helps to keep their body heat steady because the temperature of water does not vary as much as the temperature on dry land.

Crocodilians also save energy by moving about in rivers, because the water supports their heavy bodies. However, crocodilians can walk many miles on dry land. Young crocodilians may even gallop if they need to move quickly.

Aboriginal Creation Myth
Crocodiles are often shown in bark paintings and rock art made by the Aboriginals of Australia. Their creation myth, called the dream time, tells how ancestral animals created the land and people. According to a Gunwinggu

story from Arnhem Land, the Liverpool River was made by a crocodile ancestor. The mighty crocodile made his way from the mountains to the sea, chewing the land as he went. This made deep furrows, which filled with water to become the river.

▲ **ALL-AMERICAN GATOR**
American alligators can be found on the southeastern coast of the United States, especially in Florida and Louisiana. The population of alligators cannot spread further north than Virginia or further west than Texas because the winters are too cold.

▲ **RIVER DWELLERS**
The gharial is a type of crocodilian that likes fast-flowing rivers, such as the Indus in Pakistan and the Ganges in India. It prefers rivers with high banks, clear water and deep pools where there are plenty of fish.

◄ CROWDED POOL

Caimans are a type of crocodilian from South America. During the dry season, they gather in the few remaining pools along drying-up river beds. Although the pools become very crowded, the caimans seem to get along well. In some areas, caimans are forced to live in river pools for four or five months of the year. After the floods of the wet season, they can spread out again.

SUN-LOVING NILE CROCODILES ►

These Nile crocodiles bask on the river banks to warm themselves after a night in the water. If they get too hot, they simply open their mouths and the evaporation from their huge mouths soon cools them down. If they still feel too hot, they simply slide into the water. Despite their name, these crocodiles live around many African lakes and rivers, not just the Nile.

◄ SHALLOW SWAMPS

This swamp is a billabong — a branch of a river that comes to a dead end. Billabongs provide crocodiles with water and land as well as food to eat. This one, in the Northern Territory of Australia, is home to Johnston's crocodiles. They lurk in shallow water, waiting to snap at fish, reptiles, birds and small mammals.

Saltwater Crocodiles

Most crocodilians live in fresh water, but some individuals venture into the salty water of estuaries (river mouths), and a few wander out into the sea. The species most likely to be seen at sea is the saltwater or estuarine crocodile. This is the world's biggest crocodile, and it grows up to 20 feet in length. It is found over a vast area, from India to northern Australia. Saltwater crocodiles are usually found in coastal rivers and swamps, but some have been seen swimming hundreds of miles from land. Some populations live entirely in the sea, and come ashore only to lay their eggs.

Living in salt water causes a problem for crocodiles. As they eat their food they swallow sea water, but they cannot cope with too much salt in their bodies. Crocodiles therefore have salt glands on their tongue that get rid of the extra salt.

▲ GETTING RID OF SALT
Saltwater crocodiles have up to 40 salt glands on the tongue. These special salivary glands allow the crocodile to get rid of excess salt. Freshwater crocodiles also have these glands, perhaps because their ancestors lived in the sea. Alligators and caimans do not have salt glands.

SCALY DRIFTER ▶
Although it can swim vast distances far out to sea, a saltwater crocodile is generally a lazy creature. Slow, side-to-side sweeps of a long, muscular tail propel it through the water, using as little energy as possible. Saltwater crocodiles do not like swimming vigorously, so they avoid strong waves wherever possible. They prefer to drift with the tide in relatively calm water.

NEW WORLD CROC ▶

The American crocodile is the most widespread crocodile in the Americas, ranging from southern Florida, to the Pacific coast of Peru. It is usually about ten feet long, although some grow up to 20 feet. The American crocodile often lives in brackish (slightly salty) water. It can be found in swamps, estuaries and lagoons as well as in rivers.

◀ TRAVELING CAIMANS

A group of baby spectacled caimans hides among the plants. This wide-ranging species lives mainly in muddy rivers but can tolerate salt marshes. Many caimans live on islands in the Caribbean, which their ancestors probably reached by swimming through the sea or by clinging to drifting logs.

◀ LOST ARMOR

A saltwater crocodile has less protective armor on the neck and back compared to other crocodilians. This makes it easier for the crocodile to bend its body when swimming. Thick, heavy scales would weigh it down too much at sea.

▲ ADVENTURE AT SEA

Nile crocodiles typically live in rivers, but they also inhabit salty estuaries. A strong current may sometimes sweep a crocodile out to sea. Some crocodiles survive these unplanned journeys and reach inhabitable islands.

Open Habitats for Birds of Prey

Many birds of prey make their home on grassland, moorland and other stretches of open land. Each species has adapted to a particular kind of habitat and to hunting the prey that is found there. This prevents too much competition for the food resources available. Imperial and golden eagles hunt in mountainous country. The gyrfalcon and snowy owl are the most successful predators on the bleak expanses of the Arctic tundra. Farmland provides a hunting ground for kestrels and harriers, while the vast savanna lands of eastern and southern Africa are the home of many vultures. Here, there are rich pickings on the carcasses of zebras and antelopes killed by large predators. Many vultures also hunt small prey themselves.

▲ **GROUND NESTER**

A young Montagu's harrier spreads its wings in the nest. Like other harriers, it nests in vegetation on the ground. This harrier lives on open moors and farmland throughout Europe, northern Africa and Asia.

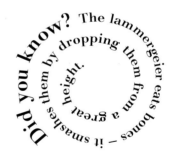

Did you know? The lammergeier eats bones – it smashes them by dropping them from a great height.

◄ **TUNDRA HUNTER**

A gyrfalcon devours its prey. This bird lives in the cold, wide-open spaces of the Arctic tundra, in Alaska, northern Canada and northern Europe. The picture shows a young bird with dark, juvenile plumage. The adult is much paler – gray above and white underneath. Some birds are almost pure white and blend in perfectly with their snowy habitat.

▲ VULTURES AT THE CAPE

The Cape vultures of southern Africa inhabit the clifftops and hilly regions around the Cape of Good Hope. They have broad wings that enable them to soar effortlessly on the warm air currents rising from the hot land below. Often, several birds soar high in the air together, watching out for a meal to share.

▼ KILLING FIELDS

A common buzzard feeds on a dead rabbit that it has found. Buzzards live in open and lightly wooded country throughout the world. They can be found in both lowland and upland areas where their food — mainly small mammals — is plentiful.

◄ PLAINS WALKER

The secretary bird of Africa's savanna grassland is the only bird of prey that walks in search of prey. Its long legs enable it to search in all but the tallest grass, and the bird usually kills its prey by stamping on it.

▼ SUNNING ON THE SAVANNA

A young bateleur eagle suns itself on a tree in the savanna of Africa. When fully grown, it will fly over the grasslands all day, keeping a watchful eye for prey such as small mammals and reptiles.

bateleur eagle
(*Terathopius ecaudatus*)

Birds of Prey in Woods and Near Water

honey buzzard
(Pernis apivorus)

The world's forests make good hunting grounds for many different kinds of birds of prey. The goshawk and sparrowhawk, and the common and honey buzzards, all make their homes in woodlands. Many owls prefer to live in woods, too. The most formidable forest predators, however, are the enormous South American harpy eagle and the Philippine eagle. They live in rainforests and prey on monkeys high in the treetops.

Lakes, rivers and estuaries are the territory of the sea and fishing eagles and the osprey. They have rough scales on their feet to help them grip slippery fish. In Asia and Africa, the fishing owls make their homes in woodlands close to the coast or by inland waterways.

▲ FOREST FEEDER

The honey buzzard is quite a small bird, found in the forests of Europe. Its bill is small and delicate compared to other raptors, well suited to its diet of the larvae of bees and wasps.

◀ IN THE MARSHES

Three marsh harrier chicks peep out of their reed nest in a swampy region of Poland. This species is the largest harrier, measuring up to 21 inches from head to tail. Marsh harriers glide over reed beds and open farmland to hunt. They are fearsome predators that eat birds, small mammals and reptiles.

◄ DOWN IN THE JUNGLE

The harpy eagle lives in the dense forests and jungles of Central and South America. It is an awesome predator, picking animals as big as sloths and monkeys from the trees, as well as birds such as parrots. Harpy eagles grow up to 3 feet from head to tail. They have huge talons that can grip heavy prey.

▲ DAYLIGHT OWL

Hawk owls live mainly in the forests of the far north, where there is permanent daylight in the summer. They usually sit on a perch and dart out to catch prey.

▼ EAGLE AT SEA

The white-bellied sea eagle lives high on the clifftops of an island in Indonesia, Southeast Asia. Like other sea eagles, it takes fish from both coastal and inland waters and also feeds on carrion. This eagle will even eat poisonous sea snakes.

▲ FLEET FLIER

The sparrowhawk is found in the woodlands of Europe and Asia. It flies swiftly and close to the ground, using the dense vegetation as cover. However, it sometimes hunts like a peregrine, circling high and then diving steeply at its prey.

Horses of the World

There are no truly wild horses any more, but feral herds are found all over the world. Feral horses are the descendants of tame horses that escaped from people. They run wild without any human interference. Semi-wild horses also run free, although these horses are owned by people and are sometimes rounded up to be tamed. Horses can live in many different habitats because their main food, grass, grows in most open areas.

The relatives of horses — asses and zebras — are less widespread. Zebras are found only in Africa, south of the Sahara Desert. Wild asses live in scattered areas of eastern Africa and Asia. Many species of wild ass and zebra are now threatened with extinction.

NORTH AMERICA

SOUTH AMERICA

◄ **OUTBACK**
Australia has the largest number of feral horses in the world. They are known as brumbies and can be found in a wide range of habitats throughout Australia. They run wild over dry plains, wetlands, grasslands and in the mountains.

▼ **SOUTH AMERICA**
These feral horses live in the Falkland Islands, near Argentina. Their home is one of moorland, sand dunes and rocks.

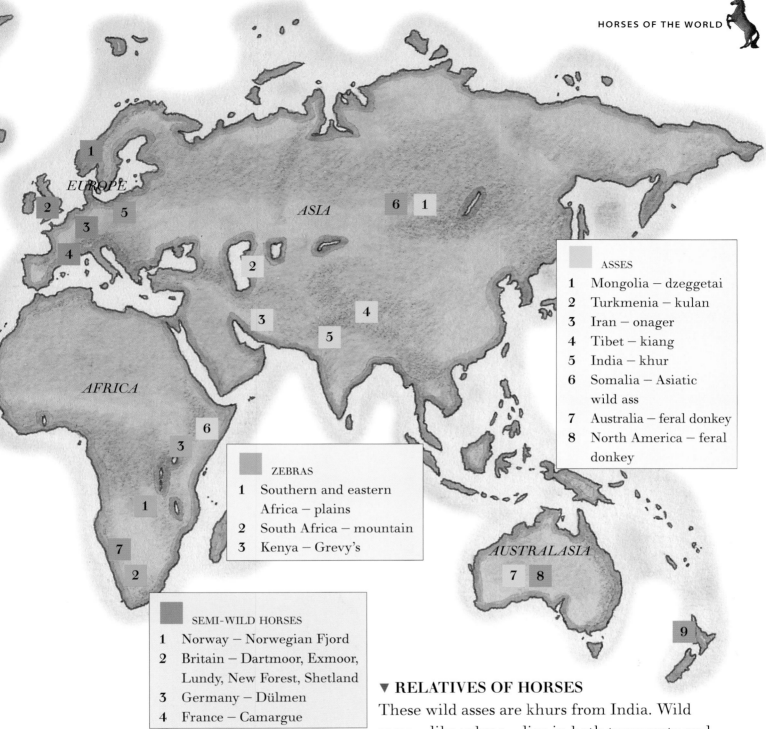

EUROPE

ASIA

AFRICA

AUSTRALASIA

ASSES

1 Mongolia – dzeggetai
2 Turkmenia – kulan
3 Iran – onager
4 Tibet – kiang
5 India – khur
6 Somalia – Asiatic wild ass
7 Australia – feral donkey
8 North America – feral donkey

ZEBRAS

1 Southern and eastern Africa – plains
2 South Africa – mountain
3 Kenya – Grevy's

SEMI-WILD HORSES

1 Norway – Norwegian Fjord
2 Britain – Dartmoor, Exmoor, Lundy, New Forest, Shetland
3 Germany – Dülmen
4 France – Camargue

FERAL HORSES

1 Western North America – mustang
2 Sable Island, Canada – Sable Island
3 Assateague Island, USA – Assateague, Chincoteague
4 Argentina – Criollo
5 Poland – tarpan
6 Mongolia – Przewalski
7 Namibia – Namib Desert
8 Australia – brumby
9 New Zealand – Kaimanawa

▼ RELATIVES OF HORSES

These wild asses are khurs from India. Wild asses – like zebras – live in both temperate and dry, tropical regions. Both species roam in small herds over open landscapes such as the savannas of Africa and the dry, rocky scrubland of Asia.

Tough Horses

WATCH THEM PLAY

Scenes such as these horses at play can be enjoyed by tourists. A blind has been set up so that people can watch the Namib Desert horses. Conservationists are divided about the horses. Some want them protected, while others want to remove them so that they do not damage the fragile desert environment.

DRINKING IN THE DESERT

Water is scarce in the desert and the horses must trek many miles to drink. These horses have started to adapt to their desert life and they are smaller than the horses from which they descended. They also urinate less, and can go without water for up to five days.

There is just one population of feral horses that has learned to survive in the desert. These horses have lived in the Namib Desert, in southwestern Africa, for over 80 years. Their ancestors were brought to Namibia by European settlers, but escaped from their owners or were released into the wild.

Horses are not natural desert dwellers, and so they have not evolved the many special features that enable other animals to thrive in hot, dry climates. The Namib horses came close to extinction in the 1970s. Just in time, people created a water supply especially for the horses. This was enough to tip the balance towards survival. Today there are about 150 horses living in the Namib Desert – one of only two or three feral groups in Africa.

of the Desert

UPS AND DOWNS OF DESERT LIFE

Namib Desert horses have survived against all odds. They live alongside specialized desert animals such as the gemsbok, ostrich and springbok.

THE NEW GENERATION

The horses breed when the rains come and food is relatively plentiful. There are few Namib horses, and they can only breed with each other because the horses live so far away from other herds. Scientists are interested in studying the effects of such inbreeding.

SAND BATHING

Horses keep their coats in good condition by rolling in sand. Namib horses are relatively free of parasites because of their isolation in a hot, dry desert. This unique environment is useful to scientists trying to understand how animals cope with extreme climate change.

ESSENTIAL RAIN

The Namib horses are thin for most of their lives, but they grow fatter and the population swells in years of good rains. The sudden growth of desert plants provides them with an instant food bonanza.

Elephant Habitats

The two species of elephant, African and Asian elephants, are divided into smaller groups called subspecies. The subspecies each look a little different from one another and are named after their habitats. Africa has three subspecies — the bush elephant of the open grasslands, the forest elephant of western and central Africa, and the desert elephant of Namibia. The main subspecies throughout South-east Asia is the Indian elephant. Asia is also home to two other subspecies, the Sumatran and Sri Lankan elephants.

▲ IN A SUMATRAN SWAMP
Sumatran elephants wade into swamps to find juicy grasses to feast on. They are the smallest of the Asian subspecies. These elephants are also the lightest in color, and have fewer pink patches than the other Asian subspecies.

ASIAN GIANT ▶
The rare Sri Lankan elephant is the biggest and darkest of the three Asian subspecies.

forest elephant
(Loxodonta africana cyclotis)

Did you know? The desert elephant is the tallest elephant in the world, at over thirteen feet high.

◀ ADAPTED FOR THE FORESTS
The forest elephant is the smallest African subspecies, and its size enables it to move easily through the trees. Elephants lose heat through their ears, so it is no surprise that this species, living in the cooler forests, has smaller ears than other elephants.

◀ SURVIVAL IN THE DESERT

The hot, dry deserts of Namibia in southwestern Africa are home to the rare desert elephant. This subspecies is very closely related to the African bush elephant, but it has longer legs. Desert elephants have to walk long distances to find food and water. Scientists think that this is why they have longer legs than any other subspecies.

ELEPHANT WORLD ▶

African elephants live in a broad band across central and southern Africa. They became extinct in North Africa around AD300. Today, Asian elephants live in hilly or mountainous areas of India, Sri Lanka, Southeast Asia, Malaysia, Indonesia and southern China. In the past, they roamed all across Asia.

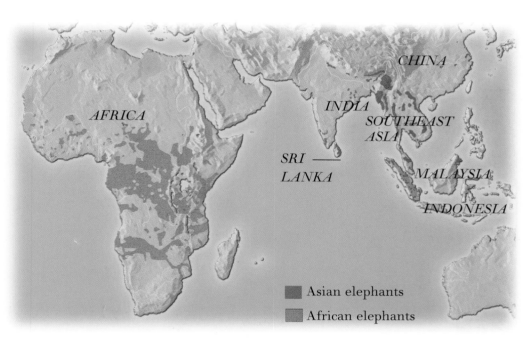

■ Asian elephants
■ African elephants

▲ IN THE SAVANNA

African bush elephants live in savanna (areas of grassland with scattered trees). Some, however, live in forests, marshes and even on mountains.

◀ SOLIDLY BUILT

The African bush elephant is bulkier and heavier than any other elephant. Like all elephants, its large size is a useful weapon against lions, tigers and other predators.

35

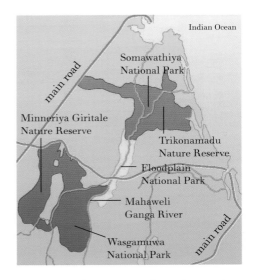

protected areas ☐ planned extension
to protected areas

▲ ANIMAL CORRIDORS

Much of Sri Lanka is used for agriculture, so elephants tend to live in protected nature reserves. They move between the regions along special corridors of land, in the same way that people travel between cities along highways.

Roaming Elephants

Like horses, elephants are constantly on the move, searching for food. They travel about 15 miles a day, ranging over a wide area.

Twice a year, elephants make long migrations to a new area to search for food and water. They gather in large groups for these journeys. The elephants follow the same paths year after year as each generation of elephants learns the route. Today, elephants have been squeezed into smaller areas as human beings take up more and more land. As a result, their migrations are much shorter than they used to be, although they may still walk for hundreds of miles.

ELEPHANT RAIDERS ▶

This corn field on the island of Sumatra lies on a traditional migration route. Elephants can do a lot of damage to crops, and farmers try to scare them away.

◀ ELEPHANT WELLS

During times of drought, elephants may dig holes in dry stream beds. They use their trunks, tusks and feet to reach water hidden under the ground. Elephants need to drink 75–95 quarts of water each day. They have been known to travel distances of up to 20 miles to reach a tiny patch of rainfall. Elephant wells can be lifesavers for other wildlife that come to drink the water after the elephants have gone.

LONG JOURNEYS ▶

African elephants on the savanna may wander over an area of more than 1,800 square miles. The extent of their migrations depends on the weather and other conditions. Asian elephants living in forests migrate over smaller areas of 60–200 square miles.

◀ **WATCHING FROM ABOVE**

Migrating elephants can be followed by airplane in open country. Little or no rain falls during the dry season and the elephants tend to group together in places where water is available. The thirsty animals usually mill around a river valley or a swamp. In rainy seasons, elephants spread out over a wider area.

◀ **PUSHING THROUGH**

Elephants will try anything to find a way through farmers' fences. They can use their tusks to break electric fence wires and even drop large rocks or logs on top of fences.

KEEPING TRACK ▶

Scientists in Africa put a radio collar on an elephant. This device tracks the animal's movements without disturbing its natural behavior.

Where Bears Live

Most types of habitat are home to a species of bear. Bears live in temperate and tropical forests, on mountain slopes, scrub desert and tropical grasslands, and on the Arctic tundra. Each species, however, has its own preferred environment. The polar bear, for example, inhabits the lands and sea ice bordering the Arctic Ocean. It favors shoreline areas where the ice breaks up as this is where its main food source, seals, gather. Most other bears are less fussy about what they eat, and have the uncanny ability to turn up wherever food is abundant. However, many of the wilderness areas where bears live are threatened. Every year, more land is cultivated for farmland and forests all over the world are cut down.

▲ IN THE BAMBOO FORESTS
The giant panda is restricted to areas of abundant bamboo forest. It was once much more widespread across eastern Asia, but now survives in just three provinces of western China – Gansu, Shanxi and Sichuan.

▼ MOUNTAIN BEAR
The spectacled bear of South America feeds on fruit and juicy leaves. It is found in humid forests as well as on open grassland and rocky areas high in the Andes Mountains.

spectacled bear
(Tremarctos ornatus)

▲ THE ADAPTABLE BROWN
The brown bear is the most widespread of all bears. It is found in Europe and the Middle East, and across northern Asia to Japan. North American brown bears, called Grizzly Bears, live in Alaska and the Rockies.

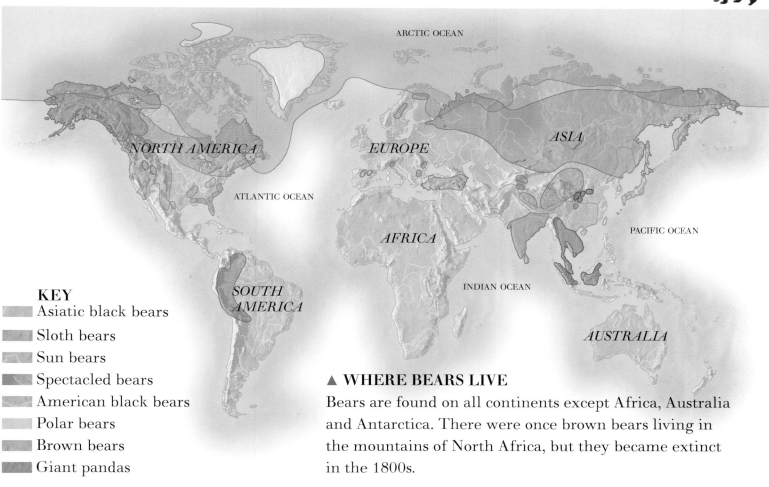

ARCTIC OCEAN

NORTH AMERICA

EUROPE

ASIA

ATLANTIC OCEAN

AFRICA

PACIFIC OCEAN

INDIAN OCEAN

SOUTH AMERICA

AUSTRALIA

KEY

Asiatic black bears

Sloth bears

Sun bears

Spectacled bears

American black bears

Polar bears

Brown bears

Giant pandas

▲ WHERE BEARS LIVE

Bears are found on all continents except Africa, Australia and Antarctica. There were once brown bears living in the mountains of North Africa, but they became extinct in the 1800s.

▲ MOUNTAIN BLACK

The Asiatic black bear lives in mountainous regions. Although related to the American black bear, Asiatic bears are smaller, perhaps because the conditions they live in are harsher.

▲ LIFE IN THE FOREST

The sloth bear lives in dense, dry forests in India and Sri Lanka. It feeds mostly at night, on leaves and fruits on the forest floor. During the day, the bear rests in a tree where it is surprisingly well camouflaged. Sloth bears are agile climbers, gripping the trees with their long claws.

Pandas in

Giant pandas live in the bamboo forests of western China. For most of the year, the panda's distinctive black and white coats stand out clearly among the greenery. But in winter, the bears become difficult to see in the snow. Some scientists believe that pandas developed their coat as a camouflage at some point in their history. They have had no reason to perfect it because there are few large predators in the areas where pandas live.

Although giant pandas are very rare – there are probably only a few hundred left in the wild – they are fairly safe as long as people do not destroy their forest homes. Habitat destruction is the largest threat to pandas.

FINDING FOOD

Bamboo forms over 99 percent of pandas' diets, although they do supplement their diet with meat when they can get it. Pandas catch rats and beetles in the bamboo, and have been known to scavenge at leopard kills. But easy prey is scarce and pandas make clumsy hunters. The abundant bamboo makes for easier picking.

THIRSTY WORK

Most of the water a panda needs comes from bamboo. If a bear is thirsty, it scoops out a hollow by a stream and drinks as much as it can. The giant panda is most active in the early morning and late afternoon. It spends 16 or more hours a day feeding.

the Bamboo Forest

ESSENTIAL FOOD

Bamboo is plentiful and easy for the bears to harvest, but digesting it is hard work. This is because the panda's digestive system is more characteristic of a carnivore. Pandas eat huge quantities of bamboo every day in order to keep going. It takes a long time for animals to evolve the perfect body to suit a new habitat.

FEEDING ALL YEAR

Even in the coldest months, bamboo is green and nutritious so the panda has a continuous supply of food. Unlike some other bears, whose food is scarce at certain times, the panda remains active throughout the winter. A thick fur coat protects it from the snow and the cold.

GOOD GRIP

A panda's front paws are specially adapted to manipulate bamboo. The wrist bones have become elongated to create a "thumb." A panda usually feeds sitting upright on its haunches. This leaves its forelegs free to handle the bamboo stalks.

Polar Bears

The polar bear is perfectly adapted to life in the Arctic, where winter temperatures can drop to -60°F. Beneath its skin lies a thick layer of fat. The bear's entire body, including the soles of the feet, is covered in insulating fur made up of thick hairs with a woolly underfur. Each hair is not actually white, but translucent and hollow. It acts like a tiny greenhouse, allowing light and heat from the sun to pass through, trapping the warm air. Sometimes, for example in zoos, the hairs are invaded by tiny algae and the polar bear's coat has a green tinge. In the wild, the fur often appears yellow, the result of oil stains from its seal prey. Beneath the fur the skin is black, which absorbs heat. This excellent insulation keeps the polar bear's body at a constant 98.6°F.

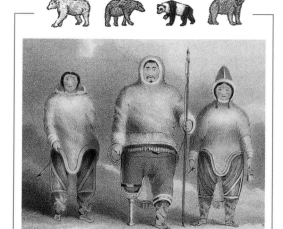

Respect for the Ice Bear
The polar bear is the most powerful spirit in Arctic cultures. The Inuit believe that a polar bear has a soul. It will only allow itself to be killed if the hunter treats it properly after death. It is forbidden to hunt another bear too soon. Time must be left for the bear's soul to return to its family. Some Inuit offer a dead male bear a miniature bow and arrow, and a female bear a needle holder.

◄ **SEA-GOING BEAR**
Polar bears are excellent swimmers. They must swim frequently because their icy world is unpredictable. In winter, the Arctic Ocean freezes over. But with the arrival of storms and warmer weather the ice breaks up. Then the bear must swim between ice floes in search of seals. The thick layer of fat below the skin and dense, insulating fur allow a polar bear to swim in the coldest seas without suffering. In such cold water, a human being would be dead in a few minutes.

▲ COOLING DOWN IN THE ARCTIC

Polar bears are so well insulated they are in danger of overheating on warm days. To keep cool, they lie flat out on the ice. At other times they lie on their backs with their feet in the air.

▲ BEAR SLUMBERS

A polar bear, like a human, sleeps for seven or eight hours at a time. This helps the polar bear to conserve energy and heat. Polar bears are not at risk of attack when they are sleeping, so they do not have to hide like other animals. Most often, polar bears find a sheltered area to protect them from the cold winds that blow across the Arctic.

▲ PROTECTED FROM THE COLD

The insulating fur and fat of a polar bear are so efficient that little heat is lost. In fact, if a scientist were to look at a polar bear with an infrared camera (which detects heat given off by the body), only the bear's nose and eyes would be visible.

CHANGING ENVIRONMENT ▶

Polar bears are most active at the start of the day. During summer, when the ice melts and retreats, bears may be prevented from hunting seals. Then they rest, living off their fat reserves and eating berries.

Cats of the Savanna

Large areas of Africa are covered with grasslands called savannas. Rain falls at certain times of the year, but there is not enough water for forests to grow. The tall grasses provide food for huge herds of antelope, zebra and other grazing animals. These in turn are eaten by many predators, which use various methods to catch the fast-moving prey. The big cats are among the most successful predators on the savannas. Lions, leopards and cheetahs all make their home on the African savanna, together with several smaller cats such as the serval. Similar grasslands in South America are home to the powerful jaguar.

▲ **CAMOUFLAGE CAT**
A lion strolls through the African savanna, its sandy coloring perfectly matching its habitat. When a lion hunts, it uses the cover of grass to hide from its quarry. It must creep up fairly close without being spotted.

This map shows where the world's tropical grasslands are located. The largest region of savanna is in Africa.

Did you know? Cats sleep for longer than most other animals. Lions sleep for 20 hours a day.

◀ **ON THE LOOKOUT**
Cheetahs are perfectly adapted for life on the plains. Here, a cheetah stands on the top of a small mound on the Kenyan savanna. It is searching for prey with its excellent eyesight. Once it spots a vulnerable animal, it races over the open, flat terrain to catch its victim. Cheetahs are the fastest of all land mammals. They can reach speeds of 70 miles per hour.

◄ VIEW FROM A BRANCH

Leopards like to live in areas of grassland where there are trees. Here they can sleep hidden during the heat of the day. They avoid the insects that live in the grass below and can enjoy the afternoon breeze. Leopards also prefer to eat in a tree, out of the reach of scavengers.

The Zodiac Sign of Leo
People born between July 24 and August 23 are born under the astrological sign of Leo (the lion). They are said to be brave, strong and proud, just like lions.

▲ AT THE WATER HOLE

During the dry season in the African savanna, many grazing animals gather near water holes to drink. Giraffes, Thomson's gazelles and zebras are shown here. Lions congregate around the water holes, not only to drink, but also to catch prey unawares. Their favorite prey animals are antelope, zebra and warthog, but they also eat young giraffes and buffalo.

SPEEDY SERVAL ►

Servals are small cats that live all over the African savanna. They like to live near water where there are bushes to hide in. The servals' long legs enable them to leap over tall grass when they hunt small rodents. They also climb well and hunt birds. With their long legs, servals can run quickly over short distances and so can easily escape from predators.

45

Forest Cats

Dense, wet rainforests are home to many insects that are eaten by birds, snakes, frogs and small mammals. In turn, these animals provide a feast for big cats. Tigers, jaguars, leopards and clouded leopards all live in rainforests, as do smaller cats including ocelots and margays. Their striped or spotted coats provide good camouflage. Forest cats hunt on the ground and in trees. They usually rest during the day and hunt at night, tracking down their prey using their superb hearing and eyesight.

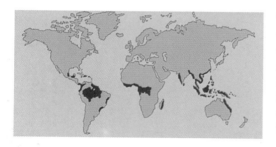

This map shows where the world's tropical rainforests are located. They lie in a band on either side of the Equator.

▲ UP IN THE CLOUDS

The clouded leopard is a shy and rarely seen Asian big cat. It lives in forests from Nepal to Borneo, spending most of its time in the trees. Clouded leopards are about three feet long with an equally long tail, and weigh about 65 pounds. They are smaller than true leopards and they can move around easily in the trees. Clouded leopards are perfectly built for climbing, with a long, bushy tail for balance and flexible ankle joints.

▼ OUT OF REACH

Leopards live in Africa and southern Asia in all kinds of habitat, from rainforest to dry grassland. They are great climbers and often drag their prey high into trees where they can be safe from thieving hyenas.

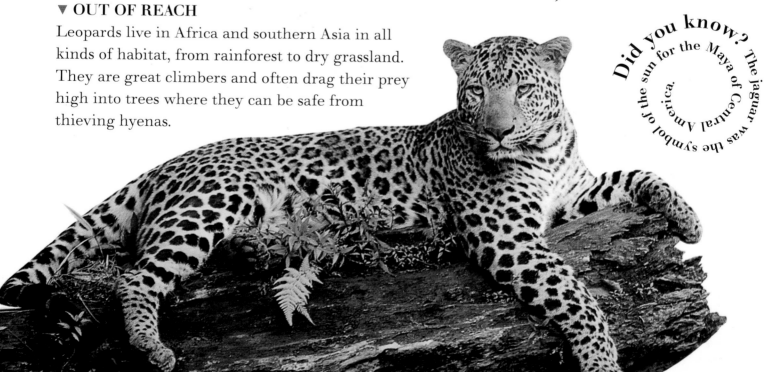

Did you know? The jaguar was the symbol of the sun for the Maya of Central America.

▲ TAKING ADVANTAGE OF THE WATER
A tiger walks stealthily into a jungle pool on the island of Sumatra. Tigers are good swimmers, and a forest pool is a good place to hunt as well as to cool off from the tropical heat. Tigers often hide the carcasses of their prey in water or in the dense undergrowth.

▲ LOSS OF HABITAT
Jaguars can be found all over South and Central America but they prefer thick forests. They are threatened by over-hunting and the destruction of their forest habitat.

▲ TOP CAT
Margays live in the tropical forests of Central and South America. They are the best of all cat climbers, with broad, soft feet and exceptionally flexible ankles and hind legs. They feed largely on birds and so need to be good at moving around in the tops of trees.

▲ A TURTLE TREAT
A jaguar catches a river turtle in a pool. Jaguars are such good swimmers that they hunt some of their prey in water. They love to eat fish and turtles. Their jaws are powerful enough to crack open a turtle's shell like a nut. They have also been known to kill caimans, a type of crocodile.

◄ LOST IN THE DARK
Forest leopards and jaguars are darker than their grassland cousins. Some are even black. The dark color helps them to virtually disappear in the shadows of their forest habitat.

Mountain Cats

To live in the mountains, cats need to be hardy and excellent rock climbers. They also have to cope with high altitudes where the air is thin and there is less oxygen to breathe. Mountain climates are harsh, and the weather can change very quickly. To survive, mountain cats need to use their wits and to know where to find shelter. They mate so that their cubs are born in the spring. This is to ensure that they will be almost grown by the time winter closes in. Big cats that live in the mountains include leopards and the rare snow leopard. Small cats include the puma, mountain cat, bobcat and lynx.

▲ **SOUTH AMERICAN CAT**
The Andean mountain cat is a secretive, shy creature and seldom seen. It is about 20 inches long and has soft, fine fur. It lives in the high Andes mountains of Chile, Argentina, Peru and Bolivia. This cat is found at altitudes of up to 16,000 feet above sea level.

This map shows the world's major mountain ranges. The puma, lynx and mountain cat live in the Americas. Lynx also live in Europe and Asia, while the snow leopard lives in Asia.

◀ **SURVEYING THE SLOPES**
A puma, sometimes known as a mountain lion, keeps watch over its vast territory. Male pumas can grow to 7 feet long, and weigh 225 pounds. They are good at jumping and can easily leap 15 feet onto a high rock or into a tree. Pumas are found over a wide area, from Canada to the very tip of South America in Chile. They live along the foothills of mountains, in forests on mountain slopes and all the way up to 15,000 feet above sea level. Depending on where they live, pumas will eat porcupines, deer, beavers, hares and armadillos.

IN THE COLD ▶
Lynx live in mountainous regions of Europe, Asia and North America. They have unusually short tails and tufted ears. Lynx are well designed to live in very cold places. In winter they grow an especially long coat, which is light colored so that they are well camouflaged in the snow.

◀ **MOUNTAIN CHASE**
A snowshoe hare darts this way and that to shake off a puma. To catch the hare, the puma makes full use of its flexible back and its long balancing tail. Pumas hunt by day as well as by night.

KING OF THE MOUNTAINS ▶
The snow leopard is one of the rarest big cats, found only in the Himalaya and Altai mountains of central Asia. It can live at altitudes of 20,000 feet, the highest of any wild cat. Snow leopards feed on wild goats, hares and marmots. Their bodies measure just over 3 feet long, with tails that are almost as long. They wrap their bushy tails around themselves to keep warm when they are sleeping. Snow leopards are agile jumpers and are said to be able to leap a gap of 50 feet. Their long tails help them to balance as they jump.

Did you know? Snow leopards are well adapted to the cold – even their feet are covered with fur.

▲ JACKAL ON ALERT
A side-striped jackal keeps a wary lookout for danger. In Africa, the three different kinds of jackal are found in different types of terrain. Side-striped jackals keep mostly to woods and swampy areas. Golden and black-backed jackals live in more open countryside.

Forest-living Wolves and Wild Dogs

Trees cover much of the world. Canada, Russia and northern Europe have many dense evergreen forests. Warmer, temperate regions contain broad-leaved woodlands. Nearer the Equator, tropical rainforests grow. In all of these areas, wolves or other species of wild dogs can be found.

Forests provide a plentiful supply of prey and dense undergrowth in which to hide and stalk. Wolves tend to live in northern regions, where large game such as deer abound. Temperate forests in Asia provide a home for the raccoon dog. Bush dogs are one of the few wild dogs to live in the rainforest. It is harder for wild dogs to survive in tropical rainforests, because most of the small prey animals live out of reach in the treetops.

◄ HIDDEN HUNTERS
In dark pine forests and dappled broad-leaved woodlands, the gray or blackish coats of wolves blend in with the shadows. This helps them to sneak up on moose, deer and other forest prey. In Arctic regions, wolves can have almost white coats, an effective camouflage in the snow.

◄ SOUND SLEEPERS

Raccoon dogs live in thickly wooded river valleys in eastern Asia. They are the only species of dog that hibernates in winter. In autumn, raccoon dogs gorge themselves on fruit and meat to put on a thick layer of fat. Then they retreat to their burrows and sleep through the harsh winter.

JUNGLE PACK ►

This wild dog is called a dhole. Packs of dholes hunt deer in the dense forests in Southeast Asia. They call to one another to surround their prey as it moves through the jungle. The pack will guard its kills against bears, tigers and scavengers.

◄ RODENTS BEWARE

Bush dogs make their home in the dense rainforests and marshlands of South America. They live close to rivers and streams, where they find plenty of animals to eat. Their main prey are aquatic rodents such as pacas and agoutis. Bush dogs will even plunge into the water to hunt capybaras – the world's largest rodents, at 4½ feet long.

A SCARCE BREED ►

A wolf surveys the snowy landscape in the Abruzzo region of central Italy. Wolves are common in remote forests in Canada and Russia, but in western Europe they are scarce. They survive in small pockets of wilderness, hiding in the hills by day and creeping down to villages to steal scraps at night.

Wild Dogs of Desert and Grassland

Wild dogs inhabit open country, as well as forests. Deserts are one of the harshest environments for wild dogs. In these barren places, the sun beats down mercilessly by day, but at night the temperature plummets. Coyotes, dingoes and foxes survive in these barren places. They can live for long periods with little water, and derive most of the liquid they need from their food. Desert foxes keep cool during the hot days by hiding under rocks or in dark burrows, emerging to hunt only at night.

Many species of wild dog live on the world's grasslands, including African hunting dogs, maned wolves and jackals.

▲ CHANGE OF COLOR

Wolves are found in deserts and dry areas in Mexico, Iran and Arabia. With little vegetation to provide cover, they stalk prey by hiding behind boulders or rocky outcrops. Desert wolves often have pale or sandy fur, to blend in with their surroundings.

▲ GIVING OFF HEAT

This jackal lives in the desert. Its large ears contain a network of fine veins. Blood flowing through these veins gives off heat, keeping the animal cool.

◀ HUNTERS OF THE OUTBACK

A pair of dingoes wait at a rabbit warren. Dingoes are descended from domestic dogs, but have lived wild in central Australia for more than 8,000 years. Their reddish-brown coats, with paler fur on their legs and bellies, are perfect desert camouflage.

▲ ADAPTING TO THE WILD

Feral dogs are the descendants of
domestic dogs that have become wild.
In Asia they are known as pariah
(outcast) dogs. Feral dogs are very
adaptable and change their behavior
to suit any situation. In India, pariah
dogs hang around villages and sneak
in to scavenge scraps.

▲ AVOIDING THE HEAT

A pack of African hunting dogs tears a carcass apart.
These dogs live on the open grasslands of Africa, which
have scorching daytime temperatures. The dogs tend
to hunt in the early morning or late evening, when it
is cooler, to avoid overheating. Gazelles and zebras are
their main prey.

The Jackal-headed God

*In ancient Egypt, Anubis, the
god of the dead, was shown
with a human body and the
head of a jackal. This god was
believed to be responsible for
the process of embalming,
which preserved the bodies of
the dead. Anubis often appears
in wall paintings and sculptures
found in burial places. Here he
is shown embalming the body
of an Egyptian king.*

▲ SLY MARSHLAND HUNTER

A maned wolf hunts in Argentinian marshland. Its long legs
help it to see over the tall grass, but it is not a fast runner.
It also lacks the stamina needed to chase prey over great
distances. Instead, it stalks animals such as rodents by slowly
sneaking up on them before making a sudden pounce.

Forest Apes

There are five species of apes: chimpanzees, bonobos, gorillas, gibbons and orangutans. They all live in Africa or Southeast Asia. Most apes inhabit tropical rainforests, but chimpanzees can be found in more open, deciduous woodlands and in wooded grasslands, and some gorillas prefer mountain forests with their lush vegetation and misty atmosphere. Gibbons sometimes live in deciduous forests, too.

All the apes used to be more widespread, but they are being gradually squeezed into smaller and smaller areas as people hunt them and destroy their habitats.

▲ **VANISHING APE**
In the dark and dappled rainforest where orangutans live, their shaggy, orange hair blends in with the tangle of forest plants. This makes them surprisingly difficult to see.

▶ **FOREST DETECTIVES**
It is often hard for scientists to watch gorillas in their wooded habitats. Instead, they study the signs left behind by the gorillas as they move about the forest.

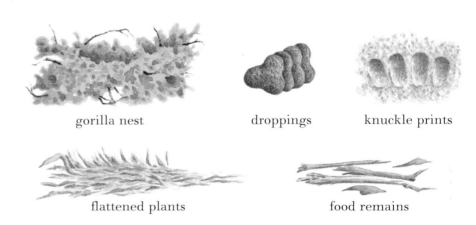

gorilla nest   droppings   knuckle prints

flattened plants   food remains

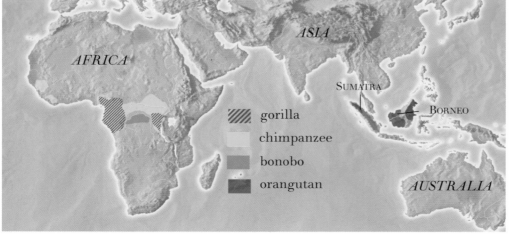

◀ **WHERE APES LIVE**
Gorillas, chimpanzees and bonobos live in Africa and orangutans live only on the islands of Borneo and Sumatra. However, orangutans once lived in parts of mainland Southeast Asia. Some people believe that they were hunted out by poachers.

ASIA

AFRICA

SUMATRA

BORNEO

AUSTRALIA

▨ gorilla
chimpanzee
bonobo
orangutan

▲ LOCAL ROUTE MAP

Chimpanzees travel around their own neighborhoods on the ground, following a network of paths. They use a mental map in their heads to decide where to go. Each day they work out where to get a good meal, climbing trees to find fruit and leaves, or to chase prey.

▲ TREETOP HABITAT

Gibbons are totally at home in the tops of the trees and hardly ever go down to the ground. They are the only apes that do not build nests. Gibbons sleep sitting up in the forks of branches, resting on tough sitting pads. These pads act like built-in cushions for the gibbon.

▲ MOUNTAIN HOMES

Dense, misty forests up to about 11,000 feet above sea level are the home of mountain gorillas. At night, the temperature sometimes drops to below freezing but the long hair of the gorillas helps them to keep warm.

▼ MAKING A COSY NEST

This chimpanzee is making a nest to sleep in. Every night, adult apes (apart from gibbons) make nests in the trees or on the ground. They bend and weave together leafy branches and pile more leaves and branches on top. This makes a warm, springy nest to keep out the cold.

chimpanzee
(Pan troglodytes)

Lowland and

It's 6.30 in the morning. A group of mountain gorillas is waking up. They are hungry after their night-time fast and reach out to pick a leafy breakfast in bed. Then the gorillas move off through the forest, feeding as they go. After a morning spent munching plants, they build day nests on the ground and take a rest for a couple of hours. This gives them time to digest their food and socialize. These gorillas live amid the beautiful and misty volcanic Virunga Mountains in Africa. They have lowland cousins who live in the tropical rainforests of eastern and western Central Africa.

CAREFUL CLIMBERS
Adult gorillas climb with great care and feel most secure when all four limbs are in contact with a branch. Young gorillas (*above*) are lighter and often play by hanging from a branch or swinging from tree to tree.

MOUNTAIN REFUGE
In 1925, the home of the mountain gorilla on the slopes of the Virunga volcanoes was declared Africa's first national park. The word virunga comes from a local expression meaning 'isolated mountains that reach the clouds.' The Virunga Mountains include both active and dormant volcanoes, but the gorillas live only on the dormant volcanoes.

SNACK IN A SWAMP
Traveling through the Odzala Forest at about 2–2½ miles per hour, these western lowland gorillas feed in a swampy glade. Like all gorillas, they walk on all fours.

Mountain Gorillas

GORILLA CHAMPION

From her hut on Mount Visoke, Dian Fossey devoted herself to studying and protecting mountain gorillas. She began her work in 1967, winning the trust of the gorillas, studying their family relationships and making discoveries about their behavior.

LIVING IN THE MIST

Mists often swirl around the forests where the mountain gorillas live, so they are called cloud forests. Mosses and lichens grow well in the cool, damp air, and hang on the branches like untidy green hair.

LOWLAND FORESTS

Eastern lowland gorillas live in the lowland rainforests of eastern Congo. It is more difficult for people to study lowland gorillas because the rainforests are less open than the mountain gorillas' habitat.

FOOD FOR FREE

On the rainy slopes where they live, the mountain gorillas have a wide variety of food, such as wild celery, bedstraw, bamboo shoots, thistles, brambles and nettles.

Mammals of the Open Sea

Whales and dolphins are mammals. Like all mammals, they breathe air and feed their young on milk. Their ancestors evolved on land, and so whales and dolphins have had to make many adaptations to live in a watery environment. They have a layer of fatty blubber beneath their skin to keep them warm, and can hold their breath for many minutes before needing to surface.

Whales and dolphins are found in all the world's oceans. Each species has a unique survival strategy to take advantage of its habitat.

◄ OCEAN WANDERER
Humpback whales migrate vast distances to find the perfect conditions for hunting and breeding.

▲ IN THE MUD
Like other dolphins that live in rivers rather than the sea, the Amazon river dolphin has a long jaw, or beak, to help it catch its prey. Its flexible neck helps it to maneuver around submerged trees and tangled vegetation in the muddy waters where it lives.

◄ WORLDWIDE KILLER
Among ice floes in the Arctic Ocean, a killer whale hunts for prey. Killer whales are found in all the oceans of the world. They live in coastal areas but may venture out to the open ocean. They also swim close to the shore, and may deliberately run aground to snatch a seal as their prey before letting the next wave wash them back to sea.

FAR NORTH ▶
A group of beluga whales swims in Hudson Bay, Canada. Belugas live around coasts in the far north of the world. In winter they hunt for fish under the pack ice in the Arctic. Belugas have a thick layer of blubber that protects them from the cold.

◀ **WARM WATERS**
These melon-headed whales prefer warm waters and are found in subtropical and tropical regions in both the northern and southern hemispheres. Melon-headed whales feed on a whole range of fish and squid, which they generally catch in deep water, well away from land.

WIDE RANGER ▶
The bottlenose dolphin is one of the most wide-ranging dolphin species, found in temperate and tropical waters in both the northern and southern hemispheres. It is also found in enclosed seas such as the Mediterranean and Red seas. When bottlenose dolphins migrate to warmer areas, they lose weight. When they return to colder climes, their blubber increases again to protect them against the cold.

Shark Habitats

Each one of the world's oceans and seas is home to at least one species of shark. Often there are many species, living at different depths and hunting different prey. Some sharks, like bull sharks, even swim in rivers and lakes. Whale, reef and nurse sharks are all tropical species that prefer warm waters. Temperate-water sharks, such as the mako, horn and basking sharks, live in water with a temperature of 50–70°F. Cold-water sharks often live in deep water. The Portuguese shark, frilled shark, and goblin shark are all cold-water sharks. A few species will swim in extremely cold waters, such as the Greenland shark which lives around the Arctic Circle.

NORTH AMERICA

ATLA OCEA

PACIFIC OCEAN

SOUTH AMERIC

▶ SWIMMING POOLS

This map shows the main parts of the world's seas in which different kinds of sharks live. The key beneath the map shows which sharks live where.

LOOKING FOR FOOD ▶

The oceanic whitetip shark lives in tropical and subtropical waters. It is one of the first sharks to appear at shipwrecks, perhaps because shipwrecks shelter lots of other fish for the whitetip to eat.

◀ ISLAND LIVING

The Galapagos shark swims in the waters of the Galapagos Islands, on the Equator. It also swims around other tropical islands in the Pacific, Atlantic and Indian oceans.

KEY

whale shark

basking shark

bull shark

tiger shark

whitetip shark

Greenland shark

great white shark

◄ UNDER THE ICE

The Greenland shark lives in deep water, and is the only shark known to survive under polar ice in the North Atlantic. It has a luminous parasite attached to each eye that attracts prey to the area around its mouth.

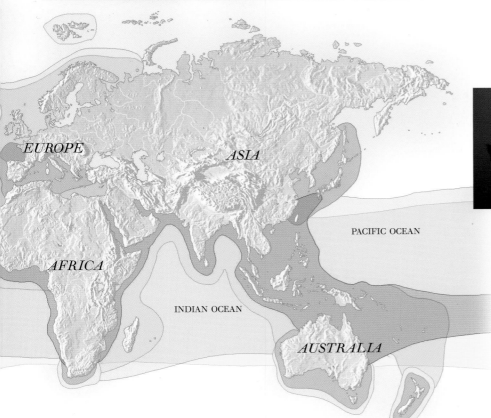

EUROPE

ASIA

AFRICA

PACIFIC OCEAN

INDIAN OCEAN

AUSTRALIA

▲ FEARSOME KILLER

The great white shark lives in temperate, tropical and sub-tropical seas. It grows to over 20 feet long and is the largest hunting fish in the seas. Its powerful jaws can bite a fully grown elephant seal (which is about 13 feet long) in half. It has strong, triangular teeth that can slice through flesh, blubber and even bone.

▲ TIGER OF THE SEAS

The tiger shark has a long, rounded shape, typical of hunting sharks. It swims mainly in tropical and warm temperate waters, both in the open ocean, and close to shore.

◄ REEF PATROL

The blacktip reef shark patrols reefs in the Indian and Pacific oceans. It also lives in shallow waters in the Red Sea and the Mediterranean, as far west as the waters off Tunisia, in North Africa.

Glossary

abdomen
The rear section of an animal's body. Inside are the reproductive organs and part of the digestive system.

adapt
To change in order to survive in changed conditions. It usually takes place over many generations in a process called evolution.

ambush
To hide and wait, and then make a surprise attack.

borehole
A hole that has been made by people to obtain water.

broad-leaved
Trees with broad, flat leaves. The term is often used to distinguish these trees from conifers.

camouflage
The colors or patterns on an animal's body that allow it to blend in with its surroundings.

canid
A member of the dog family. The group includes wolves, foxes and African hunting dogs.

carnivore
An animal that feeds on the flesh of other animals.

carrion
Remains of a dead animal.

coniferous
Trees that bear their seeds in cones. They have needle-like leaves and usually grow in cool or cold areas. Most are evergreens.

crocodilian
A member of the group of animals that includes crocodiles, alligators, gharials and caimans.

deciduous
Trees that drop their leaves for part of the year. They grow in cool, temperate areas.

environment
The conditions of an area an animal lives in.

equids
Horses and horselike animals, such as donkeys, asses and zebras.

evolution
The natural change of living organisms, usually over long periods of time, so that they become better suited to the conditions they live in.

feral
Domesticated animals that have escaped or been abandoned and are now living freely in the wild.

grassland
Open areas covered in grass.

habitat
The particular place where a group of plants or animals live.

hemisphere
One half of the Earth, divided by the Equator. The northern hemisphere lies above the Equator, the southern hemisphere below it.

hibernation
A time when body processes slow down and an animal sleeps during the cold, winter months.

insect
An invertebrate (no backbone) animal that has three body parts and six legs. Beetles, bugs and butterflies are all insects.

life cycle
The series of stages in the life of an animal as it grows up and becomes an adult.

mammal
A warm-blooded animal with a backbone. Mammals breathe air and feed their offspring on milk from the mother's body. Most have hair or fur. Whales and dolphins are mammals, although they live in the sea.

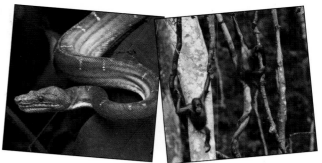

marsh
An area of land that is very wet for most of the year.

migration
A regular journey some animals make from one habitat to another, because of changes in the weather or their food supply, or in order to breed.

minibeasts
Small creatures such as insects, spiders and centipedes.

moorland
An area of open land found in cool, damp upland regions.

parasites
Animals that live on other animals and harm them by feeding on them, although they do not usually kill them. Fleas and ticks are parasites.

plain
An area of flat land without any hills.

predator
An animal that hunts and kills other animals for food.

raptor
Any bird of prey.

rainforest
A tropical forest where it is hot and wet all year round.

salt gland
An organ on a crocodile's tongue that gets rid of excess salt.

savanna
A large area of grassland in hot areas, particularly found in Africa. Savannas may have scattered trees and bushes but there is not enough rain for forests to grow.

scavenger
An animal that feeds on the remains of dead animals.

scrub
An area of land in harsh, dry areas, dominated by low-growing bushes.

semi-wild
Domestic animals that are left to run free over a large area of land for most of the year.

stagnant
Water that does not flow and is smelly. It contains very little oxygen.

steppe
A large, open area covered in grass with very few trees. Steppes are found in cool areas, especially in Asia.

subspecies
A wide-ranging species may adapt to local conditions, and look different in some parts of the world. These different forms are called subspecies, but the animals are still able to breed together if they meet.

temperate
Areas of the Earth that have a moderate climate. They are not as hot as the tropics nor as cold as the Arctic and the Antarctic.

territory
An area that an animal uses for feeding or breeding. Most animals defend their territories against others of the same species.

tropical
In the tropics, the region of the world close to the Equator, where the climate is hot and humid.

tundra
The cold, treeless land in far northern regions of the world, which is covered with snow for much of the year.

wetlands
Areas of swamps, lakes, rivers and marshy land.

Index